Poverty

Poverty

Lisa M. Bolt Simons

Living in AMERICA

CREATIVE EDUCATION

CREATIVE PAPERBACKS

Published by Creative Education and Creative Paperbacks
P.O. Box 227, Mankato, Minnesota 56002
Creative Education and Creative Paperbacks are imprints of The Creative Company
www.thecreativecompany.us

Book design by Graham Morgan (www.bluedes.com)
Art direction by Tom Morgan
Edited by Jill Kalz

Images by Getty (Alison Wright, Avalon, DenisTangneyJr, Keystone-France, Mario Tama, Ted Streshinsky Photographic Archive, Universal History Archive), The New York Public Library (Public Domain), Unsplash (Jon Tyson, Matt Collamer), Wikimedia Commons (Bernhard Gillam, Carl Weis, Dorothea Lange, FDR Presidential Library & Museum, Fibonacci Blue, J. Carwitham, Lewis Hine/NARA, Reverend Jacob H. Hooker, Shawn Miller/ Library of Congress, Social Security Administration History Archives, U.S. Department of Agriculture)

Library of Congress Cataloging-in-Publication Data
Names: Simons, Lisa M. Bolt, 1969– author.
Title: Poverty / by Lisa M. Bolt Simons.
Description: Mankato, Minnesota : Creative Education and Creative Paperbacks, [2025] | Series: Living in America | Includes bibliographical references and index. | Audience: Ages 12–15 | Audience: Grades 7–9 | Summary: "A social studies title for young adults that examines the history and effects of poverty in the United States of America, as well as safety net assistance programs. Includes sidebars, real-person profiles, a glossary, a timeline, and further resources"—Provided by publisher.
Identifiers: LCCN 2023046972 (print) | LCCN 2023046973 (ebook) | ISBN 9781640269101 (library binding) | ISBN 9781682774601 (paperback) | ISBN 9798889890782 (ebook)
Subjects: LCSH: Minimum wage—United States—Juvenile literature. | Poverty—Juvenile literature. | Poor—Services for—United States—Juvenile literature. | United States—Economic conditions—Juvenile literature.
Classification: LCC HC110.P6 S556 2025 (print) | LCC HC110.P6 (ebook) | DDC 339.4/60973—dc23/eng/20231012
LC record available at https://lccn.loc.gov/2023046972
LC ebook record available at https://lccn.loc.gov/2023046973

Printed in China

UNEMPLOYED
BUY
APPLES
5

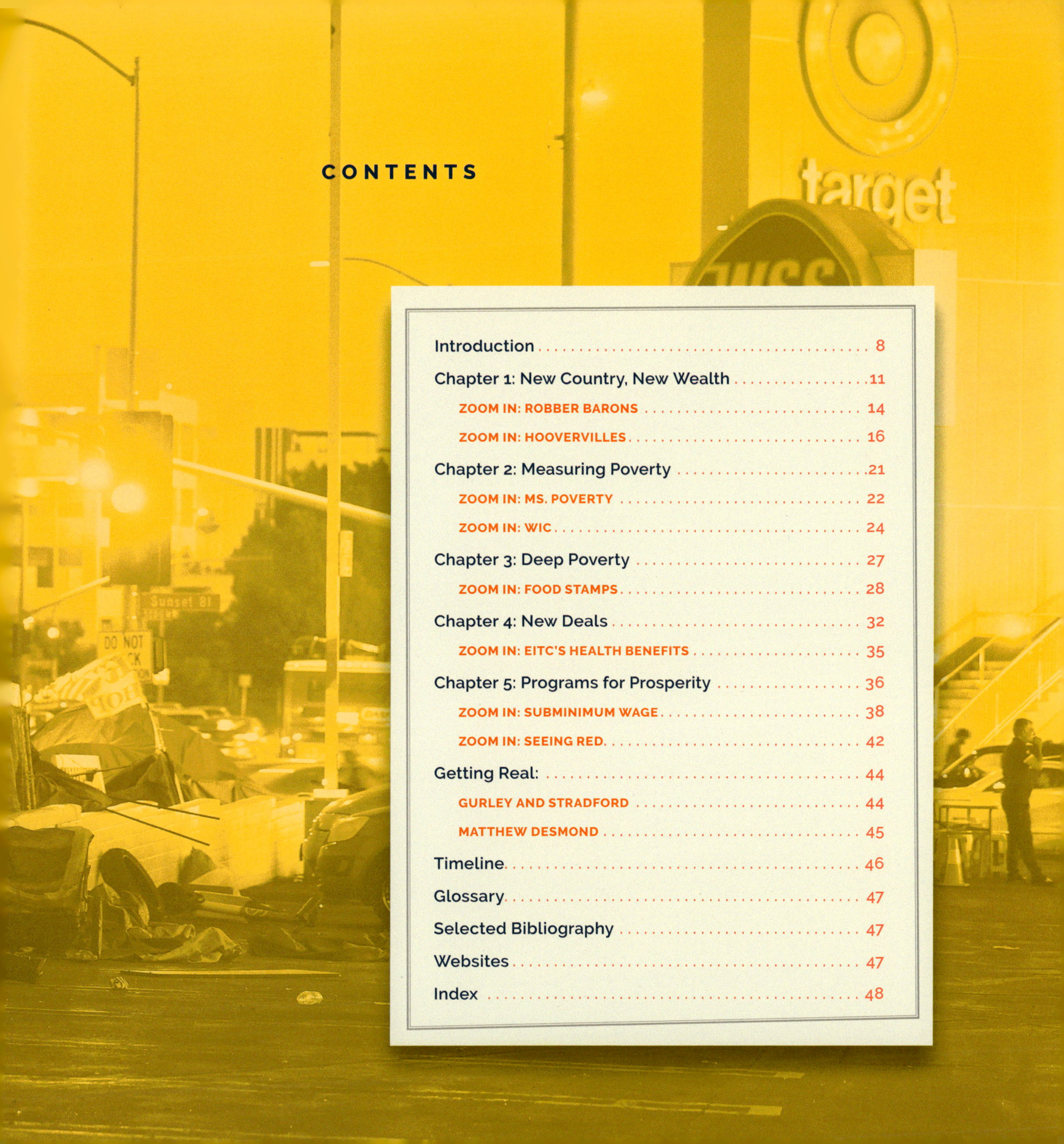

CONTENTS

Introduction

On April 24, 1964, an unemployed Kentucky coal miner named Tom Fletcher was asked if he'd like to meet the president of the United States. Fletcher said he would. Hours later, President Lyndon Johnson squatted next to Fletcher on the porch of the three-room, coal-heated house Fletcher had bought for $100 (about $1,000 in current dollars). The two men talked about Fletcher's life and how he was supporting his wife and eight children on $400 a year. Johnson wanted to use his position as president to do something about poverty and its effects on the country.

The United Nations defines poverty as "more than the lack of income and productive resources to ensure sustainable livelihoods. Its manifestations include hunger and **malnutrition**, limited access to education and other basic services, social **discrimination** and exclusion, as well as the lack of participation in decision-making."

Although Johnson's 1964 Economic Opportunity Act did provide various social programs that targeted poverty, the United States is still fighting the war today. In 2021, the U.S. Census Bureau estimated that the poverty rate was 12.8 percent. In other words, more than 42 million Americans didn't make enough money for constant access to food, education, health care, transportation, and other resources.

The United States is one of the richest countries in the world. How can anyone be living in poverty? The answer is rooted deep inside the nation's complex history, especially the treatment of its citizens.

The prospect of wealth brought people to the Americas, as depicted in this illustration of colonial Boston in the early- to mid-1700s.

CHAPTER 1:

New Country, New Wealth

The accumulation of wealth in the United States began in the 1600s, when the country was still a group of **colonies** ruled by Great Britain.

Some early colonists made their money from trading tobacco, animal skins, and other goods with Great Britain. Over the next 200 years, traders, lawyers, landowners, private bankers, and other businessmen became the wealthiest citizens. By 1843, the United States had 20 millionaires. Then came the Civil War (1861–65), tearing the nation apart. Business owners who lacked **ethics** reaped the benefits of a country in chaos. From cheaply made uniforms to rotten food, these businessmen cared only about making money. By the end of the war, New York City alone had more than 100 millionaires.

After the Civil War, some people became quite wealthy in the industry business. The country was in rebuilding mode. Steel manufacturing, electrical power, oil companies, and railroads boomed. The middle class grew. The working class did, too, as industries hired laborers to fill the many jobs. Millions of **immigrants** and people from rural areas made up this working class. But even as the United States developed and thrived, the rich got richer, and the poor stayed poor. Some workers didn't work year-round, and when they did work, their pay was low. Low pay for workers also meant more profits for business owners. By 1890, the wealthiest 1 percent of the population held 51 percent of the real estate and personal property of the United States.

Businesses and cities were growing rapidly. People increasingly moved to cities, lured by flashy promises of money and success. These people were mostly from rural areas and other countries. Reality set in, however, when low-paying factory work demanded long hours and dangerous work conditions.

In the early 1900s, things were not going well for the working class. It is believed that 1 in 3 people living and working in cities faced food insecurity. There were few city services, so living spaces were crowded. Water systems and water quality were poor. Disease spread easily. Without better-paying jobs and social services, it was not easy to move out of the city **slums**.

It was even harder for the 15 million immigrants who moved to the United States in search of a better life. In their home countries, there were rising taxes and job and food shortages. There were cruel governments. Some immigrants came to the United States because they heard it had money, jobs, healthy environments, and food. Most of them didn't know English. In addition, their cultures were quite different from that of the United States. For some immigrants,

At the turn of the 20th century, many city-dwelling Americans lived in cramped, unsanitary spaces.

FIVE POINTS.

ZOOM IN: ROBBER BARONS

In the decades that followed the end of the Civil War, businesses expanded and thrived. From dealings in oil, cotton, tobacco, railroads, banks, and steel, businessmen grew incredibly wealthy. Within this group were "robber barons." These unethical businessmen found ways to have total control of their businesses by using threats, trickery, and violence. They treated workers poorly and unfairly to boost their profits, and they didn't pay attention to their customers. Their wealth allowed them to build massive homes, decorate with European furnishings, wear designer clothes, and host extravagant parties.

their appearance added to the challenge, such as the darker skin and hair of the Italians or the smaller-looking eyes and black hair of the Chinese. They were often bullied and abused by Americans, even though the immigrants usually worked jobs Americans didn't want.

U.S. cities became more crowded, resources were scarce, and too many people couldn't get ahead financially. Then, in 1914, war broke out in Europe. The United States wanted to stay out of it, but they helped the Allied forces of Russia, France, and Great Britain with weapons and supplies. Over the next three years, the fight continued. The United States finally joined the war on April 6, 1917.

During World War I (1914–18), the U.S. economy did well. The Allied forces were buying war-related goods, which stimulated businesses and brought in money. As U.S. citizens joined the military, workers had to replace them, which meant the unemployment rate dropped from 7.9 percent to 1.4 percent. After the war, the United States started investing money internationally. For some Americans, things were looking bright. The roaring 1920s saw more people living in the cities than in the country. Homes got electricity. Manufacturers started making and distributing goods on a large scale. Car ownership exploded. And the nation's wealth more than doubled.

But not everyone was celebrating in the 1920s. Some Americans grew poorer. More than 50 percent of U.S. families made less than $2,000 a year (roughly $30,000 in today's dollars). Black Americans and immigrants were faced with violence from a racist group called the Ku Klux Klan. Black people also faced Jim Crow laws that forced them to work for low wages. After producing the huge amounts of food that were needed during World War I, farmers were stuck with too much post-war supply and no one to sell it to.

Then came October 1929—the start of the Great Depression. In 10 weeks, **stocks** lost half their value. Businesses failed, and unemployment skyrocketed. When banks failed, families lost their savings. Many people had already been living lean, and the Great Depression pushed them over the edge. Thousands of Americans lost their homes and started living in cardboard shacks across the United States. Hunger and malnutrition affected many families.

In the fall of 1932, Franklin Delano Roosevelt won the U.S. presidential election by a landslide. The opposite of the previous president, Herbert Hoover, Roosevelt wanted his administration to help American citizens. Over the next several years, Roosevelt's New Deal was rolled out. The emergency relief programs helped with home mortgages, business loans, and employment. There were banking reform laws and farming programs. A second New Deal included union protection programs to help employees keep their jobs and get fair wages. Other programs helped farmers and migrant workers. The Social Security Act was established. This program took money out of a person's paycheck and put it into a retirement fund.

New Deal programs didn't help *all* Americans, however. Black people and immigrants were still discriminated against, especially in the southern states. Jim Crow laws, started in the late 1890s, still held firm. These laws separated the races and prevented Black people from obtaining decent homes and jobs because of discrim-

ZOOM IN: HOOVERVILLES

As more and more people lost their homes around the nation during the Great Depression, they turned to basics for shelter. They built shanties out of cardboard, lumber, glass, tar paper, old bricks, or whatever they could find. Some families dug holes in the ground and put scraps of wood or paper over the top as temporary roofs. These shanty towns at the edges of big cities became known as "Hoovervilles" because people blamed the then president, Herbert Hoover, for what had happened. Hoover believed people should help themselves and not rely on the government to solve their problems.

The Great Depression forced many Americans to seek shelter in cardboard shacks.

ination. "Whites Only" and "Colored" signs were widespread at restaurants and stores and on buses and trains, as well as water fountains and restrooms. Between 1936 and 1967, Black travelers depended on the *Negro Motorist Green Book* to find safe places to stay, gas stations to fill up, and grocery stores to buy food as they crossed the country.

Despite the government's efforts, the Great Depression pushed into the early 1940s. Then, on December 7, 1941, Japan bombed Pearl Harbor, Hawaii. President Roosevelt signed the Declaration of War against Japan the next day, and the United States entered World War II (1939–45).

When millions of American men and women left to serve their country overseas, fellow citizens stepped up at home to help the war effort. Approximately 17 million new jobs were created. Those people still hurt by the depression were now able to work and save some money. Tragically, though, people of Japanese descent, even those born in the United States, were sent to **internment** camps. So were many people of German and Italian descent. Although the war ended in 1945, these interned people were not released until three years later. As a result, they were not able to work or save money.

Larger families, especially those of color, struggled to secure basic needs during the Great Depression.

Once the war ended, the United States was better off financially than it had been before the war. Many white male veterans used a government benefit called the GI Bill to buy homes and farms and to attend college. Even though Black veterans were supposed to benefit from the GI Bill, too, ongoing discrimination shut them out of housing and education opportunities throughout the country. This meant people of color and women needed to fight even harder in the decades following the war to earn their civil and financial rights.

By the mid-1960s, 18 percent of Americans were living in poverty. President Johnson launched his "War on Poverty" in 1965. Government programs helped widows, retirees, people with disabilities, students, and schools. At the same time, **poverty thresholds** were established by the Social Security Administration (SSA).

Today, the U.S. Census Bureau provides updates on the poverty rate. The rate has ranged from 11.1 percent (1973) to 22.4 percent (1959). However, this rate does not include unhoused people.

CHAPTER 2:

Measuring Poverty

From 1963 to 1964, an employee of the SSA named Mollie Orshansky created the first poverty threshold.

Orshansky based her threshold on the cheapest food plan developed by the Department of Agriculture and multiplied the costs by three. She knew that a family of three or more people spent about one-third of their money after taxes on food. Orshansky divided the thresholds into the following:

- **family size**
- **farm/nonfarm status**
- **sex of the head of the family**
- **number of children in the family**
- **elderly or not (one- or two-person families only)**

This information generated a grid of 124 thresholds and was used to define poverty.

Mollie Orshansky did pioneering work for the SSA from 1958 to 1982.

The following year, the SSA worried that perhaps the poverty thresholds needed to change as the **standard of living** increased. In 1968, the SSA tried to raise the levels, but the Bureau of Budget didn't allow it. However, there was some consideration regarding changes in the price of goods and how they affected a family's budget.

In 1973, it was decided that the poverty thresholds should be reviewed every 10 years. Yet, it wasn't until 1981 that changes were made. "Nonfarm" was applied to all families, "female-headed" and "male-headed" were removed, and the largest family size was changed to "nine persons or more." As a result, the number of poverty thresholds changed from 124 to 48.

The U.S. Census Bureau updates the poverty thresholds each year. These are used mainly to determine the number of Americans who are living in poverty. Poverty is also measured by using poverty guidelines. These are issued by the Department of Health and Human Services (HHS). There are three tables: one for the 48 states and the District of Columbia, one for Alaska, and one for Hawaii. The cost of living is higher in Alaska and Hawaii, so they have separate tables. By way of example, in Minnesota, for a two-person household, the poverty guideline in January 2023 was $19,720. In Alaska, the poverty guideline for the same parameters was $24,640. There are no defined guidelines for U.S. territories such as Puerto Rico and the U.S. Virgin Islands.

ZOOM IN: MS. POVERTY

Mollie Orshansky started working for the U.S. Children's Bureau in 1936 as a junior statistical clerk and took graduate courses in economics and statistics. After World War II, Orshansky got a job responding to letters from families asking how they could make ends meet. She and her coworker offered advice on how to create budgets and plan low-cost meals. In February 1958, Orshansky started working for the Social Security Administration. While creating poverty thresholds, she didn't have to imagine what it would be like to be poor. As the daughter of Ukrainian-Jewish immigrants who spoke little English, she remembered going with her mother to get extra food for her family.

In the 1960s, mobile services brought basic necessities to communities in need.

Several health and wellness assistance programs use poverty guidelines to determine if families can participate in them. Poverty guidelines go by the year the guidelines are established instead of every year.

Income thresholds play a role in determining poverty, too. The income used before taxes includes:

- **earnings**
- **unemployment compensation**
- **workers' compensation**
- **Social Security**
- **supplemental security income**
- **public assistance**
- **veterans' payments**
- **survivor benefits**
- **retirement income**
- **bank interest**
- **dividends or bonuses**
- **rent**
- **royalties**
- **income from estates**
- **trusts**
- **educational assistance**
- **alimony and child support**
- **assistance from outside the home**
- **other sources**

ZOOM IN: WIC

In 1968, a group of doctors met with the Department of Health, Education, and Welfare. They were concerned about pregnant women who came to their clinics sick. The doctors felt these women were either not eating nutritious food or not eating at all. They created a plan to build grocery stores attached to clinics in neighborhoods where the women could get prescriptions for food. In 1972, the Special Supplemental Food Program for Women, Infants, and Children was established as a two-year program. By 1975, this program became permanent. The program changed its name from "Food" to "Nutrition" in 1994 but is referred to as WIC.

Sheltering in unsafe, abandoned buildings may be the only choice for people living in extreme poverty.

To determine if a family is living in poverty, analysts first determine the family's poverty threshold for that year. Then, they determine the family's total income and compare it with the threshold. If the total income is greater than the poverty threshold, the family is not considered to be living in poverty.

Somebody in TEXAS Loves Me

CHAPTER 3:

Deep Poverty

According to the U.S. Census Bureau, "deep poverty" is when a household is below 50 percent of poverty thresholds. For example, if the 2023 poverty threshold for a family of four is $30,000, a family living in deep poverty would make less than $15,000 a year.

The World Bank defines deep poverty another way: living on $2.00 a day, or less, per person. What sets people living in deep poverty apart from others in poverty is that they are more likely to stay in their situation.

In 2021, 6 percent of the U.S. population lived in deep poverty. As a percentage, this may not sound like a lot. But it's equal to more than 20 million people. Those with a greater risk of falling into deep poverty are individuals and single-mother families. About half of those mothers are under the age of 25. American Indian and Alaska Native people are most likely to live in deep poverty. In 2021, their rate was 10 percent. The rates for Black people and Latinos were 9.3 percent

Families led by a single mother are at greater risk of falling into deep poverty.

ZOOM IN: FOOD STAMPS

The first food stamp program in the United States ran from 1939 to 1943. It allowed people to buy orange stamps valued at $0.25 each for what they normally spent on food. Fifty cents of blue stamps were given for $1.00 of orange stamps. In other words, an unemployment check for $2.00 would get a person $2.00 in orange stamps, plus $1.00 in blue stamps. Orange stamps could buy any food, while blue stamps were used to buy extra food as determined by the Department of Agriculture, such as eggs, flour, or beans. The first food stamp program reached about 20 million people around the country.

and 7.9 percent respectively. Least likely to live in deep poverty in 2021 were white people and non-Latinos, at 3.9 percent.

Very often, life circumstances make digging out of deep poverty extremely difficult. Most adults in this situation haven't worked for a year or more. They may have drug or alcohol addiction issues. They may have a disability or a long-term illness. People in deep poverty may be unhoused or living in unsafe neighborhoods. Maybe they've been in jail. Perhaps they can't find good childcare that would allow them to go out and work.

Children under the age of 18 make up a larger percentage of the deep poverty number than adults. More than 7 percent of all children in the United States lived in deep poverty in 2021. More specifically, more than 10 percent of children ages 6 and younger lived in deep poverty households.

When children live in deep poverty, there are both short-term and long-term effects. Short term, deep poverty can affect brain development and body functions. The situation can also put children at risk for having poor health or recurring illnesses. A baby born into a poor family is in a

F.S.C.C.
F.S.C.C.
25 CENT
NON-TRANSFERABLE
SURPLUS FOOD ORDER
SUBJECT TO CONDITIONS
PRESCRIBED BY THE SECRETARY
OF AGRICULTURE
25
25

F.S.C.C.
F.S.C.C.
25 CENT
NON-TRANSFERABLE
FOOD ORDER
SUBJECT TO CONDITIONS
PRESCRIBED BY THE SECRETARY
OF AGRICULTURE
25
25

AHEAD

Makeshift encampments are home to those in deep poverty who have nowhere else to go.

worse situation than a child who first experiences poverty at age 5 or 6. Being in deep poverty for more than half of one's childhood often leads to malnutrition. Families buy cheaper food, which tends to be processed, less healthy, and lacking in fresh fruits and vegetables. This situation can result in obesity, which can lead to health problems such as heart disease, strokes, type 2 diabetes, and some cancers.

Long term, researchers claim that girls who grow up in deep poverty are more depressed and anxious, while boys grow up to be angrier. There's a higher chance that these girls and boys will not graduate from high school. They may also have children of their own while still teenagers. As adults, they'll likely not have steady work, housing, or other reliable resources. Because those born into deep poverty are less likely to succeed in major stages of life, the cycle of that deep poverty will most likely continue.

The question of why anti-poverty programs haven't helped those most in need is a tough one. Researchers think it's because those programs aren't geared for people who are in too deep. For example, one cash assistance program has mandatory work requirements. But suppose you're on your way to work, and your car breaks down. You don't have the money to fix your car, and you can't get to work to make the money to fix your car or to meet the requirements for assistance.

A family living in deep poverty can get housing assistance. But what if that family can't find childcare? Children can't be left alone while their parents work. Without regular work, how can that family afford food? Food insecurity can be a major concern for deep poverty households.

There are also people who have mental or physical issues who don't qualify for disability benefits. Yet, because of the issues, they can't find or hold a steady job. If assistance programs expect people to work regularly, these individuals are stuck and can't get out of the vicious cycle.

CHAPTER 4:

New Deals

The U.S. government has tried several assistance programs through the years to combat poverty and help its citizens.

Some of the New Deal programs established by President Roosevelt in the 1930s are still around today, including Social Security. This assistance program takes money out of an employee's paycheck and puts it into a fund. That fund gets distributed to the employee upon their retirement. Social Security is a major source of income for retirees and those who have lost their spouse. It also helps people with disabilities, as well as their family members. In addition, Social Security helps children under the age of 18 if their parents die. In 2017, the program helped 62 million Americans, distributing $955 billion.

Included in the Social Security Act of 1935 was unemployment insurance. This insurance helps workers who become unemployed and meet certain criteria. It's based on federal law, but each state runs its own program. Funds are meant to help with living expenses until people can return to regular work.

U.S. president Franklin D. Roosevelt's New Deal programs helped improve the lives of many people during the Great Depression.

When President Johnson declared his War on Poverty with his 1964 Economic Opportunity Act, he included Head Start. This preschool program was designed to help break the cycle of poverty. It helped fulfill not only the educational needs of low-income children but also their emotional, social, nutritional, and health needs.

The Supplemental Nutrition Assistance Program (SNAP) was also started in 1964. Nearly 60 years later, in 2023, this food stamp program served 42 million people with more than $62 billion in benefits. Studies show that SNAP helps increase baby birth weights. In addition, researchers in Michigan determined that the number of deep poverty households with children is cut by 50 percent if SNAP benefits are included in household income. In 2018, SNAP saved more than one million children from deep poverty.

In 1965, two important health care programs were added: Medicare and Medicaid. Medicare is for people over the age of 65 and for people who have certain diseases or disabilities. It provides health insurance for people with low incomes. Approximately 55 million people received more than $615 billion in benefits in 2015. Both the federal government and the states fund this program, but the money comes from taxes. Medicaid is for children in low-income families. In 2015, approximately 68 million children were in this program.

Three assistance programs were added in the early 1970s. The Supplemental Security Income Program (SSI) gives cash to people with low incomes who are age 65 or older, as well as to those who have a disability. The Women, Infants, and Children (WIC) program helps pregnant women, new mothers, and young children in low-income households who need help with their nutrition. And Pell grants help low-income college students pay their tuition and other costs. According to the 2022–23 grant guide, family incomes needed to be $49,999 or less to qualify.

ZOOM IN:
EITC'S HEALTH BENEFITS

Created in 1975, the Earned Income Tax Credit (EITC) was designed to help families living in poverty. Although the EITC isn't a health care program, research has shown that this source of extra income positively affects the health of families. In families taking the EITC, mothers generally schedule health check-ups before the baby is born. As a result of these pre-natal visits, the mothers' health, and the health of their babies, is better monitored. There are also lower rates of smoking and drinking for pregnant mothers receiving the EITC, resulting in better mother and baby health.

In 1975, the Earned Income Tax Credit (EITC) program was added. Benefiting working people, especially families, it provides a tax break for those with low to moderate income. In 2015, more than 46 million people took advantage of the EITC. Fortunately, because this tax credit is not considered income, it does not count against other assistance, such as SNAP.

The Temporary Assistance for Needy Families (TANF) program was established in 1996. It now includes the Tribal TANF. Both programs issue federal grants to states. These grants give benefits to help families with children—but with a five-year limit. Job preparation, family planning, and healthy marriage and relationship education are the focus.

In 1997, the Children's Health Insurance Program (CHIP) was established to provide low-cost coverage to children. At the time, nine million children were without health insurance. Families couldn't afford private insurance, but their incomes were also too high to qualify for Medicaid. Twelve years later, the CHIP Reauthorization Act strengthened the program. Funding was added, improvements were made, grants were earmarked for American Indians, and enrollment was promoted for both CHIP and Medicaid. In 2016, CHIP cost the federal government $15 billion.

The most recent federal program designed to fight poverty is the Affordable Care Act (ACA). It was put into place by President Obama in 2010. It includes government assistance to help people with low incomes pay for health insurance. It also helps states pay for more low-income families' Medicaid by providing matching funds. With exploding health care costs, assistance is especially critical for those people living in poverty. In 2017, the total health care cost for people under the age of 65 in the United States was an astounding $705 billion.

CHAPTER 5:

Programs for Prosperity

In 1932, when President Roosevelt pledged to address the problems of the Great Depression, he believed that his New Deal programs would improve the lives of Americans. And they did, but temporarily—and not for *all* citizens.

Today, researchers, social scientists, and **grassroots** organizers have developed plans for how to reduce (or even erase) poverty in the United States. It has been suggested that the programs currently covering low-income households and families be extended to *anyone* in need. These "safety net programs" provide basic needs and stability when a person or family is experiencing hardship.

When a person loses their job, the loss can have a domino effect. They may not have money to buy food, which leads to food insecurity. Then they may get behind on rent or mortgage payments

In 1966, grape pickers in California marched to protest low wages and poor working conditions.

ZOOM IN: SUBMINIMUM WAGE

The subminimum wage is $2.13 per hour. This pay rate is for tipped workers in service industries, teens who work 90 days or less, and workers with disabilities. It began after the Civil War, when freed slaves served white patrons for a tip versus pay. It became a way to underpay Black workers who ran into discrimination while looking for other jobs. When the 1938 Fair Labor Standards Act was passed with the first federal minimum wage law, tipped workers were not included. Almost 30 years later, the base wage for tipped employees was less than half the minimum wage, due to racism and sexism.

and risk losing their home. Loss builds upon loss. States do offer unemployment insurance, but it excludes millions of people due to work requirements, previous work earnings, time spent at a job, and immigration status. These barriers, or "red tape," keep people from getting the help they need to get back on their feet. Researchers say that if safety net programs, such as state unemployment insurance and SNAP, were open to everyone and allowed for emergency situations, people would be able to recover quicker. There would be less chance of people slipping into poverty. However, not everyone thinks these programs are a good idea. Some lawmakers think it's better to limit them or cut them altogether. They feel the government is already spending too much money. They believe safety net programs encourage dependence on the government, as well as laziness.

In November 2021, President Biden's Infrastructure Investment and Jobs Act was passed in Congress. It was supposed to create two million "good-paying union jobs" over the next decade. A union is a formally organized group of employees who act together to ensure they receive a living wage, safe working conditions, health insurance, and other benefits.

While the commitment to job creation was a good step, there are a few problems that the country must still address. One is raising the minimum wage to "good-paying" level. In 2023, the federal minimum wage was $7.25 an hour, or $15,000 a year. It had been that amount since 2009. Meanwhile, executive pay had risen *1,322 percent* since 1978.

Groups of shackled prisoners, called chain gangs, were often used for hard labor, such as digging ditches and building roads.

In conjunction with raising the minimum wage, paid family medical leave and sick days need to be addressed. Too often, jobs that pay less than $11 an hour don't have these benefits. It's estimated that workers lose almost $23 billion in pay because they need to recover from an illness or stay home with a sick family member.

Another major problem with jobs in the United States is racial and gender gaps. The unemployment rate for Black people is 9.1 percent; for Latinos, it's 7.3 percent. In the workforce, they are paid about a quarter less for every dollar a white person makes. Women of color have it worse. For every $1 a white male makes, a full-time, year-round Latina worker makes $0.57. A Black woman makes $0.64. This inequity needs to be addressed.

When the Affordable Care Act was signed into law in 2010, millions of Americans were able to access affordable health care. This coverage was especially important for those with pre-existing conditions. Coverage is currently provided to more than 40 million Americans by the ACA or the law's expansion of Medicare. Studies show that people who are covered by Medicare have better financial security, don't die prematurely, and aren't evicted from their homes as often.

One of the major causes, as well as a consequence, of poverty is mass **incarceration**. The United States puts more of its citizens—more than two million—in jail than any other country in the world. Researchers estimate that poverty rates would have dropped by 20 percent since 2009 if the nation hadn't put so many people behind bars. The communities most affected by this statistic are those of color. Black men are six times more likely to be incarcerated than white men; Latinos are more than twice as likely.

Having a loved one in jail puts a financial burden on the family. Income is reduced, sometimes for years. Once the person is released, they will often have a

I.

hard time finding a job and housing, as well as accessing assistance programs they may have had before. Therefore, lawmakers and other decision-makers need to focus on finding alternatives to incarceration. For example, including mental health agencies, social workers, and community care experts during a crisis can sometimes help a person avoid jail time. If the person does end up in jail, "clean slate laws" may help reduce or eliminate hurdles to jobs, housing, education, and assistance, especially for those with minor or decades-old offenses. Wherever possible, the goal should be to help people avoid a life of poverty. In the long run, it only benefits society as a whole.

Research has shown that connecting with a child from the day of birth to age two or three is crucial. Reaching out to new mothers at the hospital and parents during home visits, especially those mothers who are experiencing after-birth depression, are important intervention steps. Although taking care of a family can be expensive, poor health, incarceration, or losing one's job or home is, too. The more support families can get for stable and healthy lives, the more they can prevent problems—and a road to poverty—later. In addition, research shows that when babies bond with their parents, those babies are more likely to grow up to be happy, independent adults.

"Whole family" approaches to fighting poverty help adults and children at the same time. In 2016, the Obama Administration rolled out a pilot program that connected low-income families in rural and tribal areas with necessary services. While parents attended a family studies program at a local university, their chil-

ZOOM IN: SEEING RED

When the Federal Housing Administration (FHA) was established in 1934, it refused to give home loans to white families near Black neighborhoods. Maps of the time included red lines showing where whites shouldn't go. This policy became known as "redlining." Further, white families who wanted to move from these neighborhoods couldn't sell to Black families. How did the FHA justify their actions? They said property values in Black neighborhoods would decline.

dren went to Head Start. While the parents moved toward economic security, the children became more educated.

Keeping families in safe homes is a huge part of combating poverty. Yet, half the renters in the United States are spending more than one-third of their income on rent and utilities. This leaves little to cover the many other living expenses, such as food, clothing, health care, and transportation needs. Racially targeted policies have made the housing situation even worse for people of color. When renters can't pay, they face eviction. This places a lot of stress on a person or family, as the eviction can affect their chances of finding future housing. Lawmakers need to focus on programs that not only assist renters but provide them protections, as well.

Poverty is an ongoing problem in the United States and has been since the nation's earliest days. It's not certain whether new and renewed assistance programs can keep more people from slipping into deep poverty or not. Time will tell. For now, organizations, activists, and lawmakers will continue to explore options for giving workers a living wage, investing in affordable housing, and extending safety net programs. With its vast resources and wealth, the United States should be able to dismantle the culture of poverty for its citizens.

Getting Real

GURLEY AND STRADFORD

In the early 1900s, a Black neighborhood called Greenwood was established in Tulsa, Oklahoma. It was built *by* the Black community *for* the Black community. The flourishing area had grocery stores, churches, clubs, and restaurants. It had its own hospital, post office, schools, and bank. Greenwood was so prosperous that it became known as the Black Wall Street.

O. W. Gurley was one of the founders. He was born to freed slaves in Alabama. As an adult, he made his way to Tulsa, where he bought land to sell to fellow Black people. He opened a boarding house and loaned money to budding business owners.

J. B. Stradford was another Greenwood founder. The son of a former enslaved man, Stradford was a lawyer from Kentucky who moved to Tulsa to invest in real estate. He built the luxury 54-room Stradford Hotel, which was considered the largest Black-owned hotel in the country at the time.

These men and many other people worked hard, against tremendous post-Civil War resistance, to build a vibrant neighborhood. They managed to thrive despite the discriminatory laws designed to keep them down.

Then, on May 31, 1921, a mob of white men invaded Greenwood. Hundreds of Black residents were killed. The mob destroyed 1,000 homes and businesses, setting many on fire. In today's dollars, property damages totaled $27 million.

Greenwood rebuilt, without assistance from Tulsa, but the Tulsa Race Massacre took a huge toll on the spirit of the place.It also stole what could've been a bright financial legacy from future generations.

MATTHEW DESMOND

Sociology professor Matthew Desmond had a theory: If a person lost their home, that loss would affect their future economic status just as much as if they had gone to jail. He wrote about this theory in his 2016 book, *Evicted: Poverty and Profit in the American City*, which won the Pulitzer Prize and other awards. In his 2023 book, *Poverty, by America*, Desmond explored several reasons for America's poverty crisis, including tax breaks, fewer labor unions, and more personal spending. He told readers that poverty is "a national disgrace" in a country as rich as the United States and that "we need to outhate it."

When Desmond was in college, his family lost his childhood home to foreclosure. He saw the inequality around his college campus, and he felt it was confusing. Talking to unhoused people around campus also fueled his interest in poverty. Desmond blames the wealthy, not the poor, for America's situation. Because nonpoor people benefit in many ways from it, he says, poverty persists. For example, people who can afford stocks and other investments like profits. High returns are easier to realize if cheap goods and services are produced by workers with low-paying jobs.

Desmond's research focuses on housing insecurity, racial inequality, and other issues related to poverty in the United States. He believes raising the minimum wage and making it easier to form unions are two of the most important ways to fight poverty.

Timeline

1600s
American colonists start creating wealth through trade with Great Britain.

1861–65
The Civil War rips the country in two, and unethical businessmen prosper.

1890
The nation's wealthiest 1 percent hold 51 percent of real estate and personal property.

1914–18
World War I stimulates the economy.

1929
The Great Depression starts.

1933
President Roosevelt passes his New Deal programs to provide poverty relief.

1935
The Social Security Act is passed.

1939
The first food stamps are offered.

1941
Japan attacks Pearl Harbor on December 7, and the United States declares war the following day.

1963
Mollie Orshansky begins development of the first poverty threshold.

1964
The SNAP food stamps program begins.

1965
President Johnson declares his War on Poverty and debuts Medicare and Medicaid.

1972
SSI, WIC, and Pell Grants are established.

1975
The EITC is added.

1997
CHIP provides low-cost coverage to children.

2009
The minimum wage is set at $7.25.

2010
The Affordable Care Act assists with health insurance costs.

2021
President Biden's Infrastructure Investment and Jobs Act is passed.

Glossary

colony—a territory under the control of another country and occupied by settlers from that country

discrimination—applying different treatment to someone based on factors other than individual merit, such as race, gender, or income

ethics—a set of moral principles or values by which someone conducts themselves

grassroots—operating at a very basic level or foundation

immigrant—a person who comes to live permanently in a foreign country; a foreign-born resident

incarceration—confinement in jail or prison

internment—the act of being confined, especially during wartime

malnutrition—bad nutrition due to poor intake of nutrients

poverty threshold—a tool that uses a variety of factors, such as family size, to measure poverty

slum—a crowded, low-income section of a city marked by poverty and poor living conditions

standard of living—the minimum necessities and comforts that a group or area is used to having

stock—shared ownership in a company by many people who buy share, or portions, of stock, hoping the company will make a profit and the stock value will increase

Selected Bibliography

Budge, Kathleen M., and William H. Parrett. *Disrupting Poverty: Five Powerful Classroom Practices.* Alexandria, Va.: ASCD, 2018.

Desmond, Matthew. *Poverty, by America.* New York: Crown, 2023.

Ehrenreich, Barbara. *Nickel and Dimed: On (Not) Getting by in America.* New York: Picador, 2011.

Payne, Ruby K. *A Framework for Understanding Poverty: A Cognitive Approach: For Educators, Policymakers, Employers, and Service Providers.* Highlands, Texas: aha! Process, 2019.

Rank, Mark Robert. *The Poverty Paradox: Understanding Economic Hardship amid American Prosperity.* New York: Oxford University Press, 2023.

Rothstein, Richard. *The Color of Law: A Forgotten History of How Our Government Segregated America.* New York; London: Liveright Publishing Corporation, 2017.

Websites

ASPE: Poverty Guidelines

https://aspe.hhs.gov/topics/poverty-economic-mobility/poverty-guidelines

Explore this government site for details about U.S. poverty guidelines.

Drexel University: Center for Hunger-Free Communities

https://drexel.edu/hunger-free-center/research/briefs-and-reports/minimum-wage-is-not-enough

Read about the differences between minimum wage and living wage.

Index